RESISTING USURY: THE PLASTICATORS' WORKBOOK

By David C. Grossack

A Publication of Citizens' Justice Association
PO Box 390979
Cambridge, MA 02139
© 2011

INTRODUCTION

The credit card is a product of American marketing genius.

While it is arguably a necessity in many aspects, and a tremendous convenience, the credit card is essentially a financial trap.

For most Americans, it is a plastic loan shark in the wallet.

Compound interest charges accrue each time the card is used, the customer is often hardly aware of what is happening and runs up huge bills, which take years and years to reduce.

During this time, the interest keeps adding up and the bill is designed, by virtue of the constant interest, to never go away.

Add to this late fees, over-the-limit fees, membership fees, and various sleazy "promotional offers," which will be placed on your bill, and you're in hock to the plastic loan shark *for life.*

Not surprisingly, millions of consumers fall behind.

The late fees and interest pile on, and then a collection agency gets involved.

They are nasty. They are threatening. They usually disregard laws regarding fair debt collection practices, and terrorize people, often elderly, ill or laid off from jobs, into making payments.

Sometimes, the debts get sold to "debt buyers," ruthless liars who often exaggerate the debt and bully people into making more payments than they owe.

Very often, debt buyers never have the back-up documentation to prove the debt in court, and any lawyer with half a brain, or even careful pro-se litigants, can knock out their case.

Perhaps the best reason to stand up to these financial predators came in an offer the author received in the mail from First Premier Bank.

It offered a credit card at 59.95% interest, and 300,000 people signed up for it (with a credit limit of $300).

The unconscionable and vile nature of the deal is illustrated by the fact that with the credit limit being so low, customer inevitably charge over the limit and incur penalties.

Moreover, the card is designed to be used by people with bad credit, and, probably, low incomes – and thus, the payments will be late. This means, of course, late fees.

The 59.9% card is, of course, a trap, and a disgusting one at that.

Amazingly, it was preceded by a 79.9% card that was discontinued after too many collection problems.

Usury, the lending of money at interest, has been challenged by the world's major religions. But when interest rates climb higher and higher, bankruptcy is the only choice many consumers can make.

The Citizens' Justice Association has undertaken to instruct people in the technique of resisting collection efforts by the credit card industry.

We do not believe it is wrong to avoid the exorbitant interest charges from these companies. Because the economy is not a level playing field, and *tens of millions* of Americans really do not have meaningful access to the economy, we have no reservations about helping the disadvantaged resist the efforts of predators to further exploit decent people with their insidious interest gouging.

STARTING POINTS

This guide is written for those people who understand that credit card abuse can happen on both sides of the transaction.

While there are customers who spend too much and don't pay their bill, there are issuers who charge so much in fees and interest that they are engaging in credit card abuse and don't deserve a penny.

So here's how you begin to fight back (once you have decided that you are ready to):

(a)   forget your credit score
(b)   learn some law
(c)   tangle with some lawyer/bill collector

While your credit card company gives you a long contract in tiny print, saying that they can change the terms of the contract at any time, you should be able to, also.

While credit card contracts often state that they will not accept any terms and conditions on the reverse of a check (called by lawyers a "restrictive endorsement,") in fact, the fairness and reasonableness of this policy should be open to question.

Not only is the clause in fine print that nobody is reasonably anticipated to read, the credit card contract is what lawyers call "a contract of adhesion." The parties of such a contract are of unequal bargaining power and there is virtually no room for negotiation.

The credit card consumer who is fed up can send in a payment to the company with the following language put on the reverse of his or her check:

"Payee agrees to accept $10 per month on this account and to waive any and all future interest."

The payment should then be sent to the specific address mentioned in the contract for communications about your bill, not to the same address you send your bill.

A cover letter should be sent together with the check.

It should read as follows:

"Dear (Name of Bank):

I am no longer able to make the high interest payments on this account.

I believe you have taken unfair advantage of me.

I can only pay $10 a month.

By cashing this check, you agree to accept only $10 per month and to waive all further interest.

If these terms are not acceptable, please return my check.

Sincerely,

(Your Name)"

The check will not be returned.

It will be cashed.

Save it.

It is evidence that the bank arguably entered into a new contract with you called a "novation."

The theory of novation is now the cornerstone of your litigation defense strategy, if the bank decides to sue you.

WHAT READERS NEED TO KNOW ABOUT NOVATION

Thanks to some testing and research, we know that the defense of "novation" can often cause significant problems for the collection lawyers who pursue credit card debt, whether they represent the card company itself or the debt buyer.

A novation has been defined by a New York court as a "substitution of a new obligation for an old one." The elements of a novation are: (1) a previously valid obligation; (2) an agreement of all parties to the new contract; (3) extinguishment of the old contract and (4) a valid new contract supported by consolidation. (*Salim v. Schlick Landscaping* 233 NY L.J.11 (2005).

In our proposed solution, there was a previous obligation, which is generally recognized as legally valid, even though the author believes it is unconscionable when interest exceeds 18%.

There is also, I will argue, an agreement of parties to the new contract, which is evidenced by the creditor cashing checks with restrictive endorsements. The restrictive endorsement extinguishes the old contract and creates a new agreement supported by checks.

This is the controversial position which I advice people to assert, and it is not popular. When aggressively litigated, some collection lawyers have backed off, but two judges have refused to accept it.

Nevertheless, our students and clients have defeated summary judgment motions at least five or six times.

Motions for summary judgment are filed by collection lawyers who try to win the case on exhibits, affidavits and argument, saying no factual issue exists and therefore as a matter of law, the plaintiff (creditor) is entitled to a judgment without any trial.

Why have we been able to beat summary judgment motions?

Simply because there are court cases in every single state in America which say that novation is a question of fact and inappropriate for summary judgment. (See *Alexander v. Angel* (1951) 37 Cal. 2d856, 860 (236 P 2d 561).

As long as you raise the defense of novation in your answer to the complaint, you should be able to defeat summary judgment and force your opponent to trial.

Trial means live witnesses and real records have to be produced.

It may also mean you get a shot at "jury nullification."

The Significance of a Restrictive Endorsement on a Check

The reader has very likely seen checks that have unusual terms on the back. These terms can indicate that the "payee" (the person to whom the check is made out) agrees to change his telephone carrier, or have his account debited each month for a magazine, or, in commerce, to accept a check as payment in full.

The terms on the back of the check are called a "restrictive endorsement."

The Court of Appeal of Louisiana, Fourth Circuit, for example, has stated that a check with a restrictive endorsement, deposited in the ordinary course of business, can serve as a basis for accord and satisfaction, if the creditor should have reasonably become aware of the restriction and the offer of compromise is explicit. (*Didriksen v. Sewerage and Nater Board*, 527 80 2d 310 (1988)).

In *Cook v. Rebar*, a celebrated Alabama case, a dissatisfied customer of a termite control company sent the company an insert seeking to modify their contract. They also sent their renewal payment. The insert stated that acceptance of the payment and continued service would constitute acceptance of the terms of the addendum, which indicated that the parties were free to litigate any dispute.

When the customers filed suit, the company sought to compel arbitration, unsuccessfully. The company's actions cost them dearly.

The holding in the case included this statement by the court:

"Whether parties have entered a contract determined by reference to the reasonable meaning of the parties external and objective actions. Conduct of one party to a contract from which the other may reasonably draw an inference of assent to an agreement is effective as acceptance." *Cook's Pest Control, Inc. v. Rebar* 852 802d 730.

In other words, accepting payment and continuing service was acceptance.

The Uniform Commercial Code

Every state in the United States has adopted some version of the Uniform Commercial Code, which affects such legal topics as checks, sales of goods, promissory notes, and a variety of other business transactions.

Some states do not put much value in restrictive endorsements on checks unless there is more evidence that all parties agreed to the new terms. Oregon is such a state.

Other factors involved include the fact that credit card agreements usually prohibit the sending of checks with restrictive endorsements and do not obligate the company to honor the endorsement. These contracts obscure the language in print that is small and not exactly prominent.

But generally, the Uniform Commercial Code will uphold the validity of the restrictive endorsement.

Do restrictive endorsements create a novation?

I would argue yes. A novation, remember, is a new contract to replace the old one. An accord and satisfaction is a new contract.

But regardless of these distinctions, the Uniform Commercial Code will *usually* offer grounds for supporting the meaning and effect of the restrictive endorsements.

In the author's home state of Massachusetts, this is true.

Chapter 106: Section 3-311. Accord and Satisfaction by Use of Instrument

Section 3-311. (a) If a person against whom a claim is asserted proves that (i) that person in good faith tendered an instrument to the claimant as full satisfaction of the claim, (ii) the amount of the claim was unliquidated or subject to a bona fide dispute, and (iii) the claimant obtained payment of the instrument, the following subsections apply.

(b) Unless subsection (c) applies, the claim is discharged if the person against whom the claim is asserted proves that the instrument or an accompanying written communication contained a conspicuous statement to the effect that the instrument was tendered as full satisfaction of the claim.

(c) Subject to subsection (d), a claim is not discharged under subsection (b) if either of the following applies:

(1) The claimant, if an organization, proves that (i) within a reasonable time before the tender, the claimant sent a conspicuous statement to the person against whom the claim is asserted that communications concerning disputed debts, including an instrument tendered as full satisfaction of a debt, are to be sent to a designated person, office, or place, and (ii) the instrument or accompanying communication was not received by that designated person, office, or place.

(2) The claimant, whether or not an organization, proves that within 90 days after payment of the instrument, the claimant tendered repayment of the amount of the instrument to the person against whom the claim is asserted. This paragraph does not apply if the claimant is an organization that sent a statement complying with clause (i) of paragraph (1).

(d) A claim is discharged if the person against whom the claim is asserted proves that within a reasonable time before collection of the instrument was initiated, the claimant, or an agent of the claimant having direct responsibility with respect to the disputed obligation, knew that the instrument was tendered in full satisfaction of the claim.

Case law also supports the effectiveness of a restrictive endorsement in Massachusetts.

In *City Coal Co. of Springfield v. Noonan*, 434, Mass. 709, the defendant noted on his check their "endorsement and payment constitute satisfaction in full of amount due under para. (1) Judgment of 1/10/91 the endorsement was subsequently crossed out and the check cashed by the creditor.

Nevertheless, the court concluded crossing out the restrictive language was a unilateral action and ineffective.

Thus, restrictive language on the check is of legal significance and should not be lightly discounted.

In *Worcester Color Company v. Henry Wood's Sons Company*, 2001 Mass. 108 (1911A) the Supreme Judicial Court held:

> The proposition that the acceptance and collection of a check, proffered upon the condition that it is full settlement of an unliquidated claim, even though accompanied by protestation that it is not so rectified, bars any attempt to collect the balance, is supported by the great weight of authority.

Thus for over one hundred years, this has been the law in Massachusetts.

Your state may be different.

But the tools to put up a significant resistance to wear the collection lawyer down are there. Learn them and use them.

CREDIT CARD INTEREST RATES GO TO COURT

Credit card interest rates usually enjoy wide protection from usury laws.

Under a United States Supreme Court decision (*Marquette v. First Omaha Service Corp.* 439 U.S. 2990 (1978)), courts have recognized the rule that banks organized in states that allow very high limits (or no limit) on interest rates can charge the same rates in any other state as well. This is the reason many banks that issue national credit cards are based in Delaware or South Dakota.

Rosemary DeCristoforo, though, a Beverly Mass. resident, was fortunate enough to find a lawyer who thinks "outside the box."

Ms. DeCristoforo was a customer of Citibank and became late with her payments. For this reason, Citibank increased her interest rate to slightly over 54%.

When Citibank sued her to recover the money she allegedly owed them, she counter attacked, claiming that the interest rate she was charged was not usurious (as a matter of law) but *unconscionable*.

Judge Robert Cornetta of Essex Superior Court in Salem issued an opinion quite sympathetic to her, stating that interest rate charges above eighteen percent are unconscionable and so outrageous as to warrant holding them unenforceable.

Judge Cornetta's decision included some unflattering observations of the consumer credit industry.

In 2003, there were 144 million credit card holders in the U.S. While the number of cardholders has since 1990 risen by 350%, income has risen only by 188%, the judge observed, also noting that consumers are using credit cards for everyday necessities, such as food and utilities. In November 2007, total credit card debt has reached an all time high of $790.2 billion. Judge Cornetta observed that the "general public was drowning in credit card debt" and that "unregulated interest rates and hidden fees ... make it impossible for consumers to get out from under these debts, adversely impacting upon the ability of consumers to ever emerge from an endless interest and fees induced spiral."

Regrettably, Judge Cornetta's opinion is not binding on other judges. However, it can be brought to the attention of other judges and used in argument.

Citibank is not alone in charging very high interest rates. First Premier Bank, based in Sioux Falls, South Dakota, issued a credit card carrying an interest rate designated for folks with damaged credit, at 79.9 percent, again, demonstrating that the industry has little empathy for the poor, unemployed or disabled, who often are forced into these rates if they want a credit card.

A GUIDE FOR DEFENDING CREDIT CARD LAWSUITS
WITHOUT A LAWYER

You've been sued. A credit card company or a debt buyer has decided to bring you to court to recover what they are claiming is a debt owed by you. Don't roll over for them.

If you followed our suggestions, you have defenses to raise and you are not powerless.

You have an absolute right to represent yourself in court, if you choose to do so.

The right to be your own attorney is well established and has been upheld by the United States Supreme Court. See *Powell v. Alabama*, 287 US 45 (1932).

My first book, *How To Win A Lawsuit Without Hiring A Lawyer*, tells you the very basics of representing yourself without a lawyer. The key to successful self-representation is to understand the procedural rules of the court you are in. Reading that book is important to understanding the process that you are facing.

The good news is that in most states, the procedural rules mirror the Federal Rules of Civil Procedure, which are fairly straightforward.

The first step, when you are sued, is to preserve your right to fight back. You've been served with a complaint. That is a document prepared by a lawyer for the card company or debt buyer, which says that you owe them money. A sample of what one of their complaints might look like is found in our Appendix as "Exhibit A."

That document is filed in court, and they served a copy on you. If you don't file a response in the time specified on the summons (20 days in Massachusetts), the facts alleged in the complaint are assumed true. You'll be defaulted and that allows the other side to seek a judgment and execution against you... a result you want very much to prevent, because that execution is the document that allows the other side to start grabbing your real estate, paycheck and bank accounts.

If you are late, you can file a Motion to Vacate Default, but it is a hassle and there is always a chance you will have a problem in doing it, so it is best to file a response quickly and get it both to the court house, with a copy served on the lawyer who is suing you, and a copy for your file.

What should your response say?

You will be preparing a document known as an **Answer,** which must be filed in court and served on the plaintiff's lawyer. It should have the name of the court, case caption and same docket number as the complaint served on you.

On this form, you admit or deny each allegation raised in the complaint by numbered paragraphs to match the other side's. You can add replies that further explain your position. You obviously admit your name and address. But your answer must insist that the credit card agreement you entered into was substituted with a novation, and if you don't raise that defense in your answer, the defense might be considered waived. Novation is important because it tells the court you have a new contract to supplement the prior one, if it ever existed, and that there will be a material issue of fact in dispute, because novations are always an issue for a trier of fact, and you are requesting trial by jury!

A sample answer to a debt buyer's complaint is in the appendix.

It is important to raise your defenses in your answer.

The key to your defense is novation, the establishing of a new agreement, whereby the terms of your repayment are altered.

Novation has been defined as a mutual agreement among all parties to a contract for the discharge of a valid existing obligation by the substitution of a new valid obligation. *Ainsworth v. Lee,* 218 Miss. 813 (Miss. 1953). This interpretation by a Mississippi court is generally consistent with other courts around the nation. See also *Tri State Oil Tool Enterprises v. EMC Energies Inc.*, 561 P2d 714 (Wyo.1977).

Some of the defenses, in addition to novation, that you should raise include:

A. **Unconscionability.** That is, the interest charged is so high as to be outrageous, unfair and immoral, and therefore unenforceable. This defense may not prevail, but the judges will take careful notice of it, and some will be sympathetic and cut you some slack.

B. **Accord and Satisfaction.** Basically, you are defending by answering that the case has been settled already.

C. **Payment.** You've paid the amount due, i.e. your $5.00 monthly payment on your accord.

D. **Fraud In the Inducement.** You were coaxed into the deal by misleading statements or material omissions of fact.

E. **Affirmative Defenses**. You must plead certain defenses or they are waived. Fraud, illegality, accord and satisfaction, arbitration and award, discharge in bankruptcy, laches, payment, release, res judicata, statute of frauds, statute of limitations, waiver and any other matter, which tells the court that even if they have a claim, you've got these defenses.

Take special note of laches. This is a defense that tells the court that even if the card company or debt buyer is with in the legal time limits for bringing the suit, they have waited so long and you have been prejudiced and the case should be thrown out.

Very often there is confusion as when the statute of limitations begins to tick in credit card cases. Is it when you have stopped paying on time? Or is it when you were "charged off"? You were in breach as soon as you were late for the last time and then stopped paying, and that is when it is your best argument can be made.

Also, you will be asked to admit or deny whether or not you owe them the balance on your charge card. You must answer that the debt is subject to repayment at $5.00 a month consistent with the restrictive endorsement on your check, and refrain from admitting the amount due. "I owe $5.00 a month. I am unsure of the amount due until I examine certain documents which should be in the hands of the plaintiff," might be a good pro-se answer to a paragraph in the plaintiff's complaint.

Most importantly, you must demand a jury trial.

A key strategy I suggest is in a variant of what is called "jury nullification." In this case, you want the jury to nullify a usurious debt and to nullify the laws that protect usury. The banksters and possibly the judge as well, will seek to bar you from getting across the fact that you have been royally screwed by exorbitant compound interest and that they should vote their conscience, not the law, and send a message about usury. Jury nullification of credit card debt is a weapon that the Courts and collection lawyers are powerless to prevent, if it is done properly.

Even if there are laws and facts against you, the situation in its entirety may offend the jury's sense of justice so badly that they will not be able to vote against you.

But before we get to trial, you'll have certain stages to pass through:

1. **Discovery.**

At some point in time, whether you are a plaintiff or defendant, you will be interested in gathering evidence from the other side, and from witnesses. This is called DISCOVERY.

Discovery can play a decisive role in the combat between parties. The procedural rules of your state are most likely patterned after the federal rules, and the numbers in use model those rules, which for the most part are mirrored by Massachusetts rules, where the author lives.

For example, *Rule 33* allows thirty (30) questions in writing to be propounded to the other side. These questions are known as **Interrogatories**.

Interrogatories are designed to elicit admissions, or leads to admissible, helpful evidence to make your case stronger using the words of the opposition. In most states, you can ask 30 questions and obtain a reply in 45 days. If no answers are given, you can begin a default proceeding. The Appendix will contain a sample set of interrogatories to a debt buyer.

You can also request the documents and tangible objects in the possession of the opposing party by filing a **Request for Production of Documents** Pursuant To Rule 34. See our sample document request in the Appendix.

Any documents relevant to the case which are likely to be admissible as evidence in Court or lead to the discovery of admissible evidence.

For example, you may want to ask the opponents to produce a copy of the assignment of the debt from the credit card company, if the plaintiff is a debt buyer. Don't be shocked if this is a hassle for them. If they can't do it, it's the end of their case.

Consider asking for a list of shareholders of their company. This is something that they will loathe to provide as well. It is within the discretion of the judge as to whether to allow it or not.

You may want to ask for copies of all contracts, correspondence and manuals of the credit card company used to train its mail handlers, policy manuals regarding receipt of checks with restrictive endorsements, and all of your account records.

Don't be surprised if the plaintiff can't produce these documents. Many debt buyers don't have them and their case is a big bluff. They can't go to trial without these records.

In fact, if the debt buyers don't produce the documents in the number of days allowed to them under your local procedural rules, you can file "A Motion to Compel Production of Documents." The court will order them to produce the document, say, in 20 days, if you suggest that. If they don't, then file a motion to dismiss. Chances are you'll get a dismissal and the case will end. See a sample motion to compel in the Appendix.

The basic purpose of discovery is to obtain the evidence to successfully defend or prosecute a claim.

The definition of a document is quite broad. For example, it may include microfiche, computer disk, videotape and audiotape, but these should be specified in the request to be certain.

As a litigant, you also have the right to inspect premises, examine tangible objects and depose witnesses governed by Rule 30. Any party or witness may be deposed, and the usual procedure is to subpoena non-party witnesses to appear in an attorney's office to give testimony before a court stenographer.

All counsel involved and pro-se parties may cross-examine the witness.

Depositions can be used to contradict statements made by witnesses in court, as can interrogatory replies.

Depositions are mainly used to acquire evidence by asking witnesses what their knowledge is about the circumstances of a case. They can have an intimidating effect. Answers are under oath and subject to perjury laws.

At the conclusion of discovery, it is not uncommon for either party to seek to file a **Motion For Summary Judgment**. This is a pleading which asks the court to decide a case prior to trial.

Rule 56 in most, if not all states, governs motions for summary judgment. In order to obtain summary judgment, the moving party must convince the court through affidavits, exhibits and a brief that no material dispute of facts exists.

That is, in fact, a request to apply the law to facts that are so obvious or agreed to that trial would be superfluous.

Trial is usually the aim of the plaintiff but a result a defendant would prefer to avoid. Occasionally plaintiffs, especially on debt collection cases, bring motions for summary judgment.

You will defend the motion for summary judgment by submitting an affidavit and exhibits about your canceled checks, and point out the court that there has been a novation.

Many cases which could conceivably result in monetary awards for the plaintiff before a jury get knocked out in "dispositive" motions, such as a Motion For Summary Judgment.

Credit companies try to use motions for summary judgment to get your case decided before a trial is held. They must show the court that there is no material fact in dispute and only the judge's application of the law is needed. This is where you write about your case in a pleading you will serve on the other side called "Defendant's Opposition to Motion For Summary Judgment." A sample of a credit card company's motion for summary judgment and a successful opposition filed by a CMS client's attorney, (the author) are enclosed at the Appendix.

You must show the court that there are facts in dispute, especially:

1. Whether or not an accord and satisfaction, and/or a novation, exist
2. Whether the interest charged is conscionable

3. Whether you have a valid counterclaim or set off for breach of the accord and satisfaction.

If the debt buyer or credit card company attempts to bring a summary judgment motion, your defense to it will be that whether or not there is a novation is a question of fact for trial, and therefore the case cannot be decided on summary judgment. This forces the plaintiff to travel to the court, bring witnesses and documentation, and expend time, money and preparation that they are often unwilling or unable to do. Fortunately, ample precedent around the country exists to support the position that deciding if a novation exists is a question of fact. See *Lewis v. Platt,* 837 P2d (1992), *Southern Surety Co. v. Mobile National Bank,* 223 Ala 463, *Alston v. Bitely,* 252 Ark 79, *Beahm v. First Western Bank,* 2000 Ark App. Lexis 243, *Howard v. County of Amador,* 22d Cal. App. 3d 962, *Credit Bureaus of Merced County v. Shipman,* 167 Cal. App. 2d 673, *Williams v. Reed* 113 Cal App. 2d 195 (1952) *E. Martin & Co. v. Brosnan,* 18 Cal. App. 477, *Moffat County State Bank v. Told,* (Superior. Ct. of Colorado) 800 P2d 1320 *Carrano v. Shoor,*118 Conn. 86 91939) *Fontana v. Julius*, 1979 Del. Ch. Lexis 388, *Groner v. Dryer,* 256 A 2d 559, *Brick* v. *Jackson & Church,* 124 Fla 347, *Ranier Holdings v. Tatum,* 275 Ga. App. 878, *Rome Bank & Trust v. Kerce,* 140 Ga. App. 546, *Aluminum Co, of America v. Home Can,* 134 Ill App. 3d 676 *Lechtleietr v. Lechtleiter,* 330 Ill App. 517, *Boswell v. Lyon,* 401 NE.2d. 735, *W-V Enterprises v. Federal Savings and Loan,* 234 Kan. 354 (1983).

You can also raise other questions, such as whether there are disputes over billing or goods and services purchased. There is law in some states which says that you can raise issues regarding quality of services and merchandise in disputes with card companies, and also with debt buyers, who are liable for claims you would have against the card company, including tortious conduct in trying to collect the debt.

Don't forget that if the debt collectors have been rude, obnoxious and engaged in any prohibited acts in trying to collect the debt, they did so as an agent of the plaintiff! This means you may have more defenses and counterclaims against them.

The author was successful in defeating four motions for summary judgment in Norfolk County, Massachusetts brought by credit card companies when he represented clients using the CMS strategies, which included raising the defenses of novation, which essentially was a defense of accord and satisfaction. The plaintiffs argued that the court was bound by a federal pre-emption of the issue of unconscionability. Title 12 of the United States Code and the Depository Institution Deregulation and Monetary Contract of 1980 allow lending banks to "export" their interest rates across the country without fear of usury laws. But the issue of whether "unconscionability" can still be raised as a defense needs to be litigated...by you!

This is an issue which is ripe for jury nullification, discussed below.

The standardized form offered to credit card customers, the Cardholder agreement or Customer agreement is what the law calls a "contract of adhesion."

In *Steven v. Fidelity & Casualty Co.,* (1902) 58 Cal.2d. 802 the Supreme Court of California defined the adhesion contract as a "standardized contract prepared entirely by one party to the transaction for the acceptance of the other." Such a contract is usually forced on a party in a take it or leave it situation. No opportunity exists for negotiating and there is a great difference in the strength of the respective side, the stronger party forcing terms on the weaker. This definition is widely accepted across the country.

This has to be kept in mind when the credit card company tries to weasel out of the "accord and satisfaction" created by the restrictive endorsement on the reverse of the check. They may argue that such endorsements are forbidden by the card member contract. But if the contract is held to be an adhesion contract, and it certainly is one, then the terms are construed to fulfill the reasonable expectations of the customer, and the court may well side with you.

We may be encouraged by the holding in *Badie v. Bank of America,* 67 Cal. App. 4th, that the requirements of objective reasonableness and good faith supply an implied limitation on a change of term provision restricting any modification or addition to the "universe of terms" included in the original agreement.

Once the restrictive endorsement is accepted, then you must argue that there is both a novation and an accord and satisfaction contracts to settle the claim on a given schedule. By violating the terms of the settlement, and pursuing you for money after you have been paying them according to the new schedule, they have breached a contract and caused you significant aggravation, which should be compensable.

It is important to remember that a motion is simply a written or oral request for the Court to do something.

Usually, a motion is filed on a type written piece of paper under the case caption and name of the court, although sometimes motions can be made orally, or in a pinch in court in handwriting.

The motion should include affidavits, legal briefs, and exhibits to the extent needed to get your point across. Frankly, the longer, more detailed and better typed the briefs and affidavits are, the better the chances of prevailing.

Well-prepared motions frequently can intimidate the other side. Discovery disputes are a frequent source of motions. Rule 11 allows you to recover a fine for defending frivolous motions.

The opposing party may frequently stall or play games in discovery and seek to prevent evidence from getting into your hands.

Rule 37 allows for **Motions To Compel Discovery** discussed above. Failure to comply with orders to produce discovery can result in many sanctions, such as default, dismissals or fines.

Ample precedents exist to permit discovery in almost every circumstance. The Federal Rules Decisions, Federal Digest and the procedural rules themselves contain ample ammunition for arguments either way in discovery.

Rule 26(b) sets forth the grounds for discovery, and the reasons for *Protective Orders*, i.e. a **Motion For A Protective Order** to prevent abusive discovery is set forth in *Rule 26(c)*.

Rules exist to bring in parties to intervene as a party *(Rule 24)* to bring class actions *(Rules 23, 23.1)* and to substitute parties *(Rule 25)*.

How To Use "Strategic" Discovery to Achieve Litigation Objectives

On two fairly recent occasions, the author has been able to use discovery, which was uncomfortable and/or inconvenient for the plaintiff that the plaintiff agreed to dismiss the case.

The first example was in Quincy District Court in Quincy, Massachusetts. A lady we'll call "Carol" was sued by a credit card company based out of state.

After filing my appearance for her, I submitted a "Notice of Taking Deposition" of the president of the credit issuing company.

When I called up to confirm the deposition, the opposing counsel told me she was going to dismiss the case.

End of matter. Happy client. Proud lawyer.

Second example was for a fellow named "Jonathan," also sued in Quincy District Court.

Jonathan was a client of a company engaged in the credit card debt negotiation business, although they called it something else. The company used what they termed a "novation process" by sending checks with restrictions on them to the credit card issuer.

Sometime later, the issuer sold Jonathan's debt to a group of investors who are well known buyers of credit card debt.

They sued Jonathan in Quincy District Court, and Jonathan hired the author to defend him.

The author's strategy was to force the debt buyer to produce any and all documents which instructed the employees of its "predecessor in interest" i.e. the credit card issuer, how to handle checks with restrictive endorsements.

First, the debt buyer's lawyer objected to the request.

I filed a "Motion to Compel," which they rather feebly and unsuccessfully objected to. The wise and learned judge who presided over the case gave my adversary 30 days to produce the documents.

On the 29th day, my adversary called me to inform me she was dropping the case.

Happy client! Proud lawyer!

You can use these techniques to adapt them to your own needs.

For example, many times the debt buyer or credit company has hired a collection agency which was a bit "over enthusiastic" in trying to recover the debt. The rules for these collection agencies are very technical and are quite easy to break.

You can use discovery to request all of the documents, sound recordings, contact information, notes and reports generated by the collection agency in trying to collect the debt.

Don't let them kid you by saying they don't have the documents, because any documents their collection agency has is in the "scope of their control" and must be produced.

You can counterclaim against the credit card company for such things as "negligent infliction of emotion distress" or, if there is such a law in your state, "unfair and deceptive business practices" for such things as excessive phone calls, communicating a debt to a third party, leaving information about the existence of a debt on an answering machine, where others heard this (I got a thousand dollars for a client) and similar abuses.

My office has two claims going, in which a debt collector sent communication to a debtor who was already represented by me.

We have another case going where a client was sued when the statute of limitations expired, which is quite unlawful.
It is considered, among other things, "abuse of process," i.e. using the judicial system for a purpose other than which it is intended.

Naturally, you'll need to counterclaim against the credit card company if their collectors were abusive. You must remember than when a company hires an agent, and the agent does something wrong, the company is liable for the agent's wrong conduct. And of course, the collection agency is an agent of the debt buyer or credit card company.

This is only a broad overview of the most frequently used procedural rules.

Specific reference to the rules and to sample pleadings and legal precedents is vital to a full and complete understanding of the law of civil procedure. Be sure to refer to the workbook section in the Appendix.

Most likely, you will be successful in defeating the plaintiff's summary judgment motion. Then you will have to prepare a trial brief which will outline your case, including your witnesses and exhibits.

Interrogatory answers provided by your adversaries are admissible, of course. The plaintiff's explanation of how it handles the incoming checks, including ones with restrictive endorsements, may be very helpful in arguing your point to the court, especially to the effect that a large company should have the ability to screen out these checks and return them if they weren't going to accept the terms.

Your opponent will no doubt have to list its witnesses and perhaps their anticipated testimony, depending on local procedures, in the trial brief. Prepare questions carefully in advance for the opposing witnesses.

You may want to ask if they ever received any instructions from supervisors on how to handle incoming checks, including ones with restrictive endorsements.

Ask the witness what the interest rate was. In the presence of the jury, you can ask how long it would take to pay off the debt by making minimum payments. Chance are, you will never pay off the debt making minimum payments.

After you ask what the interest rate is, ask how much of the claim is principal and how much is interest. This will let the jury realize how absolutely despicable the plaintiff really is.

It is important that use the plaintiff as much as possible to make your case.

Ask the plaintiff who makes the entries on the books and records he or she has with them. If the witness is not the person who makes the entries, ask her so she can be so sure they are accurate. Object to their admissibility. Just say, "Your honor, I object to these documents, they are not supported by any evidence before this court. There is no foundation for them."

Ask the witness if she has the back up charge slips to establish the amounts as accurate. If she does not, ask her "So you are asking us to take your word for it without us seeing the charge slips that these number are accurate?"

Object again to the books and records. You never know, the court may side with you. In any event, it gives the jury a peg to hang a decision on, raising questions in their mind.

Ask the mail handler how much mail comes in to their office each day. Ask how much money comes in every day. This reminds the jury of how much power one side has, and how little you have. It may help inflame the jury against the bill collectors.

It is, as stated above, possible to use jury nullification principles to convince the jurors to side with you on the issue of the unconscionability of credit card interest and on novation, even if the opposition has arguments in the other direction. Your legal case is stronger on novation, but weaker on usury and conscionability, due to the federal pre-emption issue. That is why jury nullification techniques are important.

John Jay, first Chief Justice of the United States Supreme Court told jurors: "You have a right to take upon yourselves to judge of both, and to determine the law as well as the facts in controversy."

If jurors find a law unreasonable, they have a right to vote their conscience. See Scheflin, *Jury Nullification; The Right To Say No* Southern California Law Review, 168, 174 (1972).

John Adams, who helped the create the Declaration of Independence and who served as our second president, has been quoted as saying:

"It is not only the jurors right, but his duty... to find the verdict according to his own best understanding, judgment and conscience even though in direct opposition to the direction of the court." 1771 2 *Life and Works of John Adams,* 253-255 C.F. Adams ed. 1856.

While the court will not allow you to make an outright appeal to the jury to ignore the law regarding "traveling protection for usury," by making an emotional appeal as to the issue you can sway the jury by portraying the credit card company has heartless, greedy exploiters, which they are.

Consider the famous case of O.J. Simpson, on trial for double homicide. Legal scholars widely agree that this was a case of jury nullification. Despite the presence of significant evidence, the jury voted to acquit, apparently on the basis of inflamed passions on the jury who, on the basis of race, had suspicions and hostility to a police department which had a poor image in the African American population.

Your job, then, is to make the jurors hate the credit card companies so much, inflaming their emotions and making them understand the real issues, i.e. usury, that they vote on your side.

You can try to get in as much testimony as possible as how hard it was for you to keep up with payments, how finances caused family stress, how rude the bill collectors on the phone were, how difficult life became because of credit card debt.

You can try to ask questions like "what were the profits of your company for the last year?"

Why do you have the provision in your cardholder agreement that consumers can't change their agreement?

What does the Chief Executive Officer of your company earn?

What did you do with my check with the restrictive endorsement when you received it?

Did you show it to anyone?

Did you have any discussions about it?

Who said what to whom?

But most important of all, you have to establish that yes, indeed, there was a novation.

You must emphasize the following points.

1. There was an offer. That was contained in your restrictive endorsement on the back of your check.

2. There was an acceptance. The cashing of the check was an acceptance.

3. There was consideration. Your payment represented by the check was consideration. These are the basics of a contract.

They had the choice to accept or reject the check. They accepted it.

As a large company, they knew or should have known that checks with restrictive endorsements would be coming in, and they made a conscious decision to accept them, regardless of their own card agreement.

Thus, a decision was made to enter into a new agreement with you.

These are the points you argue, and these are the reasons you have a case worth arguing.

The jury may or may not agree with you.

If you lose, there are a number of choices you have:

1. Appeal.
2. Try to negotiate with the plaintiff.
3. Try to liquidate, reduce or reschedule your debt with a bankruptcy filing.

IF YOU WIN

If you win, you have a counterclaim, if you followed the template.

You have sued for abuse of process and breach of contract.

You have been damaged by having this lawsuit as a matter of record and by losing the time spent in defending.

You also have had some emotional distress and embarrassment from being sued.

For this reason, you have some damages that are compensable.

You may ask the judge for permission to address the jury on the issue of damages, explaining what you have endured in the defense of the case.

Time lost from work, nervous upset, strain and stress at home and all of the related damages should be explained.

You may well be awarded some money!

USE THE BANKRUPTCY LAWS IF NECESSARY TO SAVE WHAT YOU HAVE AND GIVE THE PLASTIC PREDATORS THE SHAFT

Myths And Realities About Personal Bankruptcy

There are so many misconceptions floating around about personal bankruptcy that it is difficult to decide where to start to rebut them. In the event of defeat, you may need a "Plan B".

Probably the leading misconception is that somehow it is a disgrace to be bankrupt. This author couldn't disagree more. In fact, the economic reality is that it is likely that businesses will fail, individuals will not be able to handle debt and that people will be working a good portion of their lives to make payments. Of course large companies have chosen bankruptcy time after time to deal with their problems, so it is really hypocritical that bank associations frequently warn people not to file for protection under these laws, even to the point of taking out radio commercials and issuing press releases.

Not withstanding this controversy, over a million of your fellow Americans will file for bankruptcy protection this year.

For the most part, they will be relieving themselves of a tremendous burden.

For example, the myth is that in bankruptcy you lose your home. In fact, bankruptcy laws help you save your home from foreclosure. Under what is called a Chapter 13 Plan, if you have a steady source of income, the Bankruptcy Court can appoint a Trustee to help you reschedule your overdue mortgage payments and stop any auction of your property.

Another myth is that you cannot do anything about student loans.

They don't tell you that it is possible to reduce your student loan payments to a dime on the dollar, during the life of a Chapter 13 plan.

What about taxes?

Another myth shattered. Whoever said that nothing is certain but death and taxes has never been to Bankruptcy Court. In many instances, old tax debts can be wiped out completely, under what is called a Chapter 7 filing.

Moreover, auctions by the Internal Revenue Service (IRS) or local government can be prevented by a bankruptcy filing. In fact, all debt collection activity against you ceases, and collection agencies can't interrupt your supper anymore.

The myth is still circulating that bankruptcy will destroy your credit.

While bankruptcy doesn't look pretty on a credit report, in many instances it can improve your credit worthiness. If you are carrying too much debt in proportion to your income, you will have a problem getting credit. However, if you file bankruptcy, you are not longer carrying the debt, but if you still have steady income, you may get more credit!

There are two reasons why the worry about your credit is misplaced.

First, if you are close to going bankrupt the likelihood is that you already have been late making payments. Therefore, your credit is already badly damaged and you will be paying a higher rate, even if you get credit again.

The second reason is that use of credit caused your problems in the first place. Just destroy your credit cards and be better off. Under a Chapter 7 filing, you are relieved from paying back those credit cards and their 34% compound interest charges.

Even if you file bankruptcy, you will be offered credit cards. Most experts in this field advise rejecting all offers of credit cards unless the rates are low, or paying the cards off before the end of the billing cycle to avoid accrual of interest. Human nature being what it is, this doesn't happen in most cases.

Don't jump to conclusions about bankruptcy, because if you are current with your mortgage, you may likely be able to eliminate all credit card debt and still keep your home with a well-prepared bankruptcy filing!

The foreclosure and auction notices in the newspaper each week testify to the human tragedies caused by overextending on credit and interest payments.

When financial pressures are on you, don't suffer in silence. The bankruptcy court may turn out to be your best friend

Remember, when you file bankruptcy, all collection activity against you must stop as a matter of federal law, even calling your home or mailing you letters.

Auctions, foreclosures and all lawsuits must stop when you file for bankruptcy protection. Your utilities cannot be shut off.

The bankruptcy process is best done with a lawyer who specializes in the field.

It starts by filing a simple form called a Petition and it is only two pages long. Then you have to file, within 15 days, Schedules A-J, all of which are available at a legal stationery store, and of course your lawyer will have them. It will make things quicker when you let your lawyer have a list of everything you owe, including names, addresses and account numbers as well as amounts owed, whether or not they are disputed debts, and the date they were incurred, if it is available.

If you are a homeowner, and live in a state where homestead protection is available, your lawyer may well wish for you to seek homestead protection before filing. Of course, you should have a homestead filing on your property *immediately* if you do not already. It is that important that you take time off from work, postpone everything else and get this taken care of now, before new claims or obligations present themselves. Lack of a homestead has caused many people catastrophic problems down the road that could have been completely avoided.

APPENDIX "A"

COMPLAINT

(Please Note: The complaint you answer will likely look similar to this)

COMMONWEALTH OF MASSACHUSETTS

HAMPSHIRE, ss

DANA DISTRICT COURT
DOCKET NO.

PREDATORS PORTFOLIO CORP., Plaintiff vs. DIANE DEBTOR, Defendant	))))) **COMPLAINT**))))

INTRODUCTION

This is an action brought by the purchaser of an installment credit card charge account from its original issuer for monies due and owing.

JURISDICTION AND VENUE

Jurisdiction and venue are properly in the Dana District Court as a matter of law, as the debtor resides in this judicial district and the sum in controversy is under $25,000.00.

PARTIES

1. Plaintiff has a usual place of business at 326 Central Avenue, New York City, New York.

2. Defendant resides at 27 Mark Lane, Dana, Massachusetts.

3. The plaintiff is the successor in interest to Plastic Shark Bank on defendant's credit card account.

1

CAUSE OF ACTION

4.   Defendant owes the plaintiff $8,449.20 plus costs and interest for credit card charges

due and owing since September 13, 2005 and on other dates and occasions.

5.   The total due and owing is $8,449.20.

6.   The defendant has neglected and failed to pay same.

     Wherefore plaintiff prays this court award it damages, costs, and interest.

For the plaintiff
by its attorney,

_____

Dated: November 18, 2007

APPENDIX "B"

ANSWER, COUNTERCLAIM AND JURY DEMAND

COMMONWEALTH OF MASSACHUSETTS

HAMPSHIRE, ss

DANA DISTRICT COURT
CIVIL DOCKET NO.

PREDATORS PORTFOLIO CORP.,
    Plaintiff

vs.

DARLENE DEBTOR,
    Defendant

)
)
)
)
)
)
)
)
)
)

**ANSWER, COUNTERCLAIM
AND JURY DEMAND**

Now comes the defendant pro-se and responds to the plaintiff's complaint as follows

1. Defendant neither admits nor denies the first paragraph of the plaintiff's complaint, and calls upon the plaintiff to prove same.

2. Defendant admits to the allegations of the second paragraph of the plaintiff's complaint

3. Defendant denies the allegations of the third paragraph of the plaintiff's complaint

4. Defendant denies allegations of paragraphs four and five of plaintiff's complaint.

5. Defendant admits pragraph six of plaintiff's complaint.

ADDITIONAL DEFENSES

FIRST DEFENSE
ACCORD AND SATISFACTION

Defendant states that a settlement agreement exists between the parties and therefore the plaintiff's complaint must be dismissed.

SECOND DEFENSE
NOVATION

Defendant states that the agreement referenced in the plaintiff's complaint has been subject to a novation which has replaced the agreement referenced in the plaintiff's complaint.

THIRD DEFENSE
LACHES

Defendant states that the plaintiff's complaint must be dismissed on the grounds of the doctrine of laches.

FOURTH DEFENSE
STATUTE OF LIMITATIONS

Defendant defends further and states that the plaintiff's complaint is time barred and must be dismissed.

FIFTH DEFENSE
LACK OF CONSCIONABILITY

Defendant defends further and states that the agreement between the parties is unconscionable and must be dismissed.

SIXTH DEFENSE
CONTRACT OF ADHESION

The defendant further answers and defends that if any contract existed between the parties it was an adhesion contract and voidable in all or in part.

SEVENTH DEFENSE
LACK OF PRIVITY

Defendant further answers and defends that no privity existed between the parties and therefore plaintiff's complaint should be dismissed.

EIGHTH DEFENSE
OFFSET

Defendant further states that she had an offset against the plaintiff equal to or greater than the ad damnum.

COUNTERCLAIM

1. Counterclaimant Darlene Debtor is an individual residing at 27 Maple Lane in Dana, Massachusetts.

2. Counterdefendant Predators Portfolio Corp. is a business organization located at 14 Piranha Lane, New York City, New York.

FACTUAL SYNOPSIS

3. On or about June 23, 2008 the parties entered into an accord and satisfaction affixed herein as Exhibit "A".

4. The agreement between the parties called for the plaintiff to accept payments at ten dollars per month and to reduce interest to zero.

5. The plaintiff accepted the restrictive endorsement on the terms proposed by the counterclaimant and deposited her check, establishing a contract.

6. Nevertheless, in violation of the agreement between the parties, the counterdefendant commenced this action to recover the entire alleged debt in this action.

COUNT ONE
BREACH OF CONTRACT

7. The allegation of paragraphs one through six are realleged herein and made a part of this paragraph.

8. Counterdefendant breached the contract between the parties.

9. Counterclaimant was damaged thereby.

COUNT TWO
ABUSE OF PROCESS

10. Each and every allegation one through nine above is made a part of this paragraph.

11. Counterdefendant abused process by using this proceeding for purposes other than it was lawfully intended, without a reasonable basis in law of fact.

12. Counterclaimant was damaged thereby.

   Wherefore counterclaimant prays this court:

   (a) Dismiss the plaintiff's complaint.

   (b) Award her damages, costs and interest on her counterclaim as a jury of her peers would find appropriate and just.

   Respectfully,

   _____

   Darlene Debtor, Defendant Pro-se
   27 Maple Lane
   Dana, Massachusetts. 00000

APPENDIX "C"

INTEROGATORIES PROPOUNDED
BY THE DEFENDANT TO THE PLAINTIFF

HAMPSHIRE, ss

DANA DISTRICT COURT
CIVIL DOCKET NO.

```
                                  )
PREDATORS PORTFOLIO CORP.,        )
            Plaintiff             )
                                  )    INTERROGATORIES
     vs.                          )    PROPOUNDED BY THE DEFENDANT
                                  )    TO THE PLAINTIFF
DARLENE DEBTOR,                   )
            Defendant             )
                                  )
```

1.   Identify yourself by name, employment title and business address.

2.   Please state why the plaintiff had the defendant's check (Exhibit "A") if it had no intention of honoring the restrictive endorsement.

3.   Identify and describe any written documents in the plaintiff's possession or control which instruct personnel how to handle checks with restrictive endorsements.

4.   Please state the interest rate being charged to the defendant and explain precisely how it was calculated in the instant case.

5.   Is it not true that the plaintiff received, endorsed and deposited the check affixed as "Exhibit A"?

6.   Please identify and describe each and every court case in which the defendant commenced collection action after receiving a check with a restrictive endorsement and:

      (a)   Explain how the court resolved the dispute

      (b)   State the names of parties, the name of the court, the location of the court and the docket number.

7.   Please state the consideration you paid for the defendant's account.

8   Please state whether the plaintiff and/or any of its agents have ever received claims pursuant to the Federal Fair Debt Collection Practices Act, or related causes of action.

9.   If your response to the prior interrogatory was in the affirmative, kindly:

   (a) Identify and describe each claim.

   (b) Explain how it was resolved.

10. Has your interest rate ever been challenged in any court as unconscionable or usurious>

11. If the answer is in the affirmative, please identify the name of the court, the docket number and state the results.

12. Please identify the names, addresses and phone numbers of your witnesses in this case, and describe the anticipated content of their testimony.

                              Respectfully,

                              _____
                              Darlene Debtor, Defendant Pro-se
                              27 Maple Lane
                              Dana, Massachusetts. 00000

APPENDIX "D"

DEFENDANT'S REQUEST
FOR PRODUCTION OF DOCUMENTS
AND SCHEDULE "A"

COMMONWEALTH OF MASSACHUSETTS

HAMPSHIRE, ss

DANA DISTRICT COURT
CIVIL DOCKET NO.

PREDATORS PORTFOLIO CORP., Plaintiff vs. DARLENE DEBTOR, Defendant	))))))))))

**DEFENDANT'S REQUEST FOR
PRODUCTION OF DOCUMENTS**

Now comes the defendant pursuant to Rule 34 of the Massachusetts Rules of Civil Procedure and requests that the plaintiff produce each and every document requested in Schedule "A" herein.

Respectfully,

_____

Darlene Debtor, Defendant Pro-se
27 Maple Lane
Dana, Massachusetts. 00000

COMMONWEALTH OF MASSACHUSETTS

HAMPSHIRE, ss

DANA DISTRICT COURT
CIVIL DOCKET NO.

PREDATORS PORTFOLIO CORP.,
      Plaintiff

      vs.

DARLENE DEBTOR,
      Defendant

)
)
)
)
)
)
)
)
)
)

SCHEDULE "A"

1. Each and every written agreement between the parties, or your alleged predecessor in interest.

2. Any and all credit card charge slips, statements of account and invoices relating to the defendant, Darlene Debtor in your possession or scope of control.

3. Any and all training manuals, memos, directives or other graphically recorded communications concerning the processing of checks with restrictive endorsements by mail handlers at plaintiff corporation.

4. Any and all documents reflecting any assignment of defendant's alleged debt to the plaintiff.

5. Any and all certificates of corporate vote authorizing this action.

6. Any and all records of payments made by the defendant.

7. Any internal policy or procedure manuals, memos or directives concerning checks with restrictive language.

8. Any and all documents listing the names and addresses of each and every person employed by the plaintiff who handles checks mailed to the plaintiff.

9. Any and all written communications between the parties.

      Respectfully,

      Darlene Debtor, Defendant Pro-se
      27 Maple Lane
      Dana, Massachusetts. 00000

APPENDIX "E"

PLAINTIFF'S MOTION TO COMPEL
INTERROGATORY ANSWERS AND PRODUCTION OF DOCUMENTS

HAMPSHIRE, ss

DANA DISTRICT COURT
CIVIL DOCKET NO.

PREDATORS PORTFOLIO CORP.,
    Plaintiff

vs.

DARLENE DEBTOR,
    Defendant

)
)
)
)
)
)
)
)
)
)
)

**MOTION TO COMPEL
INTERROGATORY ANSWERS,
AND DOCUMENT PRODUCTION**

Now comes the defendant and moves that the plaintiff be compelled to answer each and every interrogatory fully and truthfully (see Exhibit "A" and to produce each of the documents in Exhibit "B" herein.

Defendant states that

1.   That discovery was served on the plaintiff 45 days ago.

2.   That responses are due.

3.   That the plaintiff has neglected and failed to produce the discovery requested.

4.   That the information is sought as material and relevant to the defense, the defendant wishes to raise at trial.

5.   That the defendant will be prejudiced if the documents are not produced and the interrogatories are not answered.

Wherefore defendant pray that the plaintiff be ordered to produce the discovery within seven days or the complaint shall be dismissed with prejudice.

Respectfully,

_____

Darlene Debtor, Defendant Pro-se
27 Maple Lane
Dana, Massachusetts, 00000

APPENDIX "F

PLAINTIFF'S MEMORANDUM OF LAW IN
SUPPORT OF ITS MOTION FOR SUMMARY JUDGMENT

COMMONWEALTH OF MASSACHUSETTS

NORFOLK, ss.   DOCKET NO. ████████████
                                               ████████████ DISTRICT COURT

```
████████ BANK,                     )
           Plaintiff,              )
                                   )
v.                                 )
                                   )
████████████████████               )
           Defendant.              )
                                   )
```

PLAINTIFF'S MEMORANDUM OF LAW IN SUPPORT OF ITS MOTION FOR SUMMARY JUDGMENT

STATEMENT OF THE CASE

On or about February 2, 2006 the Plaintiff, ████████ BANK, filed a Complaint with
the ████████ District Court against the Defendant, ████████████████████. The Complaint
alleges that Defendant is indebted to the Plaintiff in the amount of Ten Thousand One Hundred
Ninety One Dollars and 43/100 ($10,191.43) for the balance owed on debt incurred from
purchases made on a ████████ credit card or revolving charge account. (See Complaint, Exhibit
A.) The Defendant was served with the Complaint on or about February 18, 2006. On or about
March 2, 2006, the Defendant filed an Answer to the Complaint with this Honorable Court
denying the Plaintiff's allegations. The Plaintiff sent billing statements and previous
correspondence between the Defendant and ████████ on March 3, 2006, in response to the
Defendant's Motion to Conduct Discovery that he filed with the Court. (See Billing Statements
and copy of original application for the ████████ Card, Exhibit B). On or about March 3, 2006
the Plaintiff propounded its First Set of Interrogatories upon the Defendant. (See Interrogatories,
Exhibit C). In Defendant's Answers to Plaintiff's First Set of Interrogatories, the Defendant

admitted to obtaining a credit card from the Plaintiff, admitted to receiving invoices for an outstanding balance on the card, and also admitted to making payments on said credit account. (See Defendant's Answer to Plaintiff's Interrogatory No. 6, Exhibit D). The second to last billing statement from November 2005 shows a balance owing of 10, 197.43. (See November 2005 Billing Statement, Exhibit E). The final billing statement from December 2005 shows a payment made on December 3, 2005 of $10.00. (See December 2005 Billing Statement, Exhibit F). The Defendant is not disputing that he received these billing statements, and therefore had notice that the balance of the account was $10,197.43, as of November 2005. The Defendant was also aware that the minimum payment due in December was $836.00. (See Exhibit E). By paying only $10.00 he failed to satisfy the minimum payment required. Furthermore, the November 2005 statement shows a credit limit of $10,000.00 on the ███████ card, alerting the Defendant of the potential addition of over limit fees to his account. (See Exhibit E). Also included in the October 27, 2005 statement, on page 2, is a clause pertaining to promotional or special rates, alerting the Defendant that these rates, if applicable, had been cancelled due to a late payment. ███████ also puts the Defendant on notice that the Annual Percentage Rates could be increased on the account, at will, by ███████ if the minimum payment is not received by the due date. (See October 2005 Billing Statement, Exhibit G). The Defendant failed to make the November payment in full when he submitted payment of $10.00 on a minimum amount due of $836.00. Thus, there are no material issues of fact in dispute and the Plaintiff is entitled to summary judgment as a matter of law on the issue of liability and damages.

FACTS

Prior to the Plaintiff filing suit, a demand letter was sent to the Defendant on or about November 2005. The Defendant requested validation of the debt and was sent documents on January 7, 2006, showing that Discover had previously validated the debt and also included was a copy of the original signed application for the ████████ card. (See ████████ Validation of Debt, Exhibit H). The Plaintiff claims the Defendant purchased goods/services on a ████████ credit card account. (See Complaint, Exhibit A). The Defendant has admitted to having a ████████ credit card, and making payments on the card, and receiving statements showing an outstanding balance on the card. (See Exhibit D). The Defendant, having been in receipt of these statements, was aware of the balance owed, the minimum payments due on the account and the consequences of failing to make these minimum payments or submitting a late payment to DISCOVER. Therefore, there are no material issues in dispute and Summary Judgment in favor of the Plaintiff should be granted.

LEGAL ARGUMENT

This court should grant the Plaintiff's Motion for Summary Judgment because the Defendant, through his Answers to Interrogatories, admits to having a ████████ card, and receiving statements on the account, thus being aware of the amount owed and how it was calculated.

"Summary Judgment" is a vehicle for resolving claim on the merits, without the necessity of a trial, if there is no genuine issue as to any material fact and the moving party is entitled to a judgment as a matter of law. Mass. R. Civ. Rule 56(c); *Community National Bank v. Daws*, 369 Mass. 550, 553 (1976). In deciding a motion for summary judgment, the Court "Must consider the pleadings, the depositions, answers to interrogatories, and admissions on file, together with the affidavits, if any." *Madsen v. Erwin*, 359 Mass. 715, 719 (1985).

The burden is on the moving party to prove by credible evidence that there is no genuine issue as to any material fact and the moving party is entitled to have judgment entered as a matter of law. *Id.* The burden of demonstrating that there is no genuine issue of material fact in relevant issue is on the moving party, even if he could have no burden on that issue if the case proceeds to trial. *Leavitt v. Mizner*, 404 Mass. 826, 832 (1987). The opposing party will defeat a motion for summary judgment by setting forth the specific facts showing a triable issue. Mass. R. Civ. P. Rule 56 (e).

The inference to be drawn from the underlying facts contained in materials considered on a motion for summary judgment must be viewed in the light most favorable to the party opposing the motion. *Attorney General v. Bailey*, 386 Mass. 367, 371 (1982); citing *Hub Associates v. Good*, 357 Mass. 449, 451 (1970), quoting *United States v. Diebold, Ins.*, 369 U.S. 654, 655 (1962). The party resisting summary judgment may not rely on its pleadings to defeat the motion for summary judgment, Mass. R. Civ. P. Rule 56 (e). Rather, the party must set forth specific facts showing that there is a genuine issue for trial.

The Defendant has set forth no specific facts by pleadings or otherwise to establish and support the existence of a genuine issue as to any material fact concerning his liability for the amount owed on his ████████ credit card account. The Plaintiff has submitted an Affidavit in Support of Plaintiff's Motion for Summary Judgment, which details and verifies that the Defendant had a ███████ credit card account, and that the Defendant owes the Plaintiff $10,191.43 as a result of purchases made on his ████████ credit card account. (See Affidavit, Exhibit I).

The Defendant has admitted that he had a ████████ card and received statements on the account showing that a balance was owed. The Defendant also made payments and purchases on such card, as shown by the billings statements. The evidence provided by the Plaintiff has met its burden for summary judgment because there is no genuine issue as to any material fact. The opposing party has not set forth any facts that would create a triable issue.

Therefore, the Plaintiff contends that there is no genuine issue as to any material fact and that the Plaintiff is entitled to Judgment as a matter of law.

WHEREFORE, the Plaintiff request that this Court grant its Motion for Summary Judgment on the issue of liability and damages.

Respectfully submitted,

The Plaintiff, by its Attorney,

APPENDIX "G"

DEFENDANT'S BRIEF IN OPPOSITION TO
PLAINTIFF'S MOTION FOR SUMMARY JUDGMENT
WITH AFFIDAVIT AND EXHIBIT

HAMPSHIRE, ss

DANA DISTRICT COURT
DOCKET NO.

FIRST PREDATOR BANK CARD OF)
SOUTH DAKOTA, N.A.)
      Plaintiff)
)
)
vs.)
)
)
DAN DEBTOR and DIANE DEBTOR,)
      Defendants)
)

**BRIEF IN OPPOSITION TO MOTION
FOR SUMMARY JUDGMENT**

FACTUAL SYNOPSIS

This case is based on a consumer dispute related to a contract for use of a charge card.

By language of the complaint, the plaintiff seeks $16,276.84 in damages for allegedly unpaid card charges.

The defendant has raised in her affidavit (Exhibit "A"), the issue of the customer agreement having been subject to novation, and accord and satisfaction.

Specifically, the defendant has made an offer to compromise supported by consideration which was accepted. The offer called for reducing the interest rate to 0% per annum. The principal is to be repayed at $10.00 monthly (Exhibit A), and Affidavit of Daniel Debtor.

A check accompanying the offer with a restrictive endorsement.

In part the defendants restrictive endorsement reads as follows:

> "This is an addendum to the terms of the cardmember agreement.
> The interest will be reduced to 0% per annum. The principal, if any,
> will be payable at the rate of $10.00 monthly..."

The defendant proceeded to pay his credit card bills at a rate of $10.00 per month in accord with this addendum.

1

In these lawsuits, they have raised the defense of novation of their contract.

Defendants have also been saddled with an Annual Percentage Rate of 30.24% because they are paying their bill slowly.

ISSUES PRESENTED

I.   HAS A NOVATION OF THE CARDHOLDER AGREEMENT OCCURRED?

II. IS THERE A MATERIAL DISPUTE OF FACTS WHICH MAKES SUMMARY JUDGMENT INAPPROPRIATE?

III. IS THE PLAINTIFF CLAIM CONSCIONABLE?

POINT I.   A NOVATION EXISTS OF THE CARDHOLDER AGREEMENT

Defendant's Agreement clearly establishes that :

(1)   An agreement existed between the parties;
(2)   The defendant, by mailing a check with a restrictive endorsement to the plaintiff, made an offere with consideration to enter into a new contract.
(3)   By cashing the check with the endorsement, the plaintiff accepted the check and therefore a new contact with new terms was formed.

Novation has been defined as a mutual agreement among all parties to a contract for the discharge of a valid existing obligation by the substitution of a new valid obligation. *Ainsworth v. Lee,* 218 Miss. 813 (Miss. 1953). This interpretation by a Mississippi court is generally consistent with other courts around the nation. See also *Tri State Oil Tool Enterprises v. EMC Energies Inc.,* 561 P2d 714 (Wyo.1977).

The facts presented by the defendant in his affidavit and exhibit indicate that a new agreement had been entered into and that the terms and conditions have been altered in accord with Exhibit A.

POINT II.   A MATERIAL DISPUTE OF FACTS EXISTS WHICH MAKES SUMMARY JUDGMENT INAPPROPRIATE.

The issue of Novation is one which cannot possibly be resolved by summary judgment. The question of whether a novation has been proved is not to be determined by the "secret thought or unexpressed intent" of any of the parties, but is to be determined by the intent as expressed by words and acts of all the parties in the light of the circumstances. *Tudor Press v. University Distributing,* 292, Mass 339 (1995).

By its very essence, novation is an issue best determined by the trier of fact where witnesses are subject to cross-examination. See *Kraus v. Whitcoimb & Kavanaugh Co.*, 240, Mass. 595 (1922).

This is also the state of the law in most jurisdictions throughout the United States. See *Lewis v. Platt*, 837 P2d. (1992), *Southern Surety Co. v. Mobile National Bank*, 223 Ala. 463, *Alston v. Bitely*, 252 Ark. 79, *Beahm v. First Western Bank*, 2000 Ark. App. Lexis 243, *Howard v. County of Amador*, 220 Cal. App. 3d. 962, *Credit Bureaus of Merced County v. Shipman*, 167 Cal. App. 2d. 673, *Williams v. Reed*, 113 Cal App. 2d. 195 (1952), *E. Martin & Co.v. Brosnan*, 18 Cal. App. 477, *Moffat County State Bank v. Told*, (Superior. Ct. of Colorado) 800 P2d. 1320, *Carrano v. Shoor*,118 Conn. 86 91939), *Fontana v. Julius*, 1979 Del. Ch. Lexis 388, *Groner v. Dryer*, 256 A 2d. 559, *Brick v. Jackson & Church*, 124 Fla. 347, *Ranier Holdings v. Tatum*, 275 Ga. App. 878, *Rome Bank & Trust* v. *Kerce* 140 Ga. App. 546, *Aluminum Co. of America v. Home Can*, 134 Ill. App. 3d 676, *Lechtleietr v. Lechtleiter*, 330 Ill. App. 517, *Boswell v. Lyon*, 401 NE 2d. 735, *WV, Enterprises v. Federal Savings and Loan*, 234 Kan. 354 (1983).

Further ample precedent exists that the restrictive endorsement on a check is sufficient to affect the legal significance of the parties' relationship.

In *City Coal Co. of Springfield vs. Noonan*, 434, Mass. 709, the defendant noted on his check their "endorsement and payment constitute satisfaction in full of amount due under para.(1) Judgment of 1/10/91 the indorsement was subsequently crossed out and the check cashed by the creditor.

Nevertheless, the court concluded crossing out the restrictive language was a unilateral action and ineffective.

Thus restrictive language on the check is of legal significance and should not be lightly discounted.

In *Worcester Color Company vs. Henry Wood's Sons Company*, 2001 Mass. 108 (1911A) the Supreme Judicial Court held:

The proposition that the acceptance and collection of a check, proffered upon the condition that it is full settlement of an unliquidated claim, even though accompanied by protestation that it is not so rectified, bars any attempt to collect the balance, is supported by the great weight of authority.

Thus for over one hundred years, this has been the law in Massachusetts.

Further, the defendants also have the Uniform Commercial Code, as incorporated in M.G.L ch. 106 Section 3-311 to bolster their position

The statute reads as follows:

Chapter 106: Section 3-311. Accord and Satisfaction by Use of Instrument

Section 3-311. (a) If a person against whom a claim is asserted proves that (I) that person in good faith tendered an instrument to the claimant as full satisfaction of the claim, (ii) the amount of the claim was unliquidated or subject to a bona fide dispute, and (iii) the claimant obtained payment of the instrument, the following subsections apply.

(b) Unless subsection (c) applies, the claim is discharged if the person against whom the claim is asserted proves that the instrument or an accompanying written communication contained a conspicuous statement to the effect that the instrument was tendered as full satisfaction of the claim.

(c) Subject to subsection (d), a claim is not discharged under subsection (b) if either of the following applies:

(1) The claimant, if an organization, proves that (i) within a reasonable time before the tender, the claimant sent a conspicuous statement to the person against whom the claim is asserted that communications concerning disputed debts, including an instrument tendered as full satisfaction of a debt, are to be sent to a designated person, office, or place, and (ii) the instrument or accompanying communication was not received by that designated person, office, or place.

(2) The claimant, whether or not an organization, proves that within 90 days after payment of the instrument, the claimant tendered repayment of the amount of the instrument to the person against whom the claim is asserted. This paragraph does not apply if the claimant is an organization that sent a statement complying with clause (I) of paragraph (1).

(d) A claim is discharged if the person against whom the claim is asserted proves that within a reasonable time before collection of the instrument was initiated, the claimant, or an agent of the claimant having direct responsibility with respect to the disputed obligation, knew that the instrument was tendered in full satisfaction of the claim.

It is likely that the plaintiff will argue that the defenses raised by the restrictive endorsement should fail due to a "lack of meeting of minds."

The argument is anticipated to be that the checks are processed in a sort of "assembly line" by a large organization whose employees cannot be expected to be aware of the nuances and significance of the restrictive endorsement.

But the opposite argument is more credible. Is it credible to believe that large and sophisticated organizations such as the plaintiffs are unaware that they will be receiving checks with restrictive endorsements and take no measures to instruct employees accordingly?

For this reason meeting of the minds should be construed from the operation of the factual pattern.

POINT III.   THE PLAINTIFF'S CLAIM IS UNCONSCIONABLE AND THUS UNENFORCEABLE

Because the interest charged is exorbitant and unconscionable, the agreement between the parties should not be enforceable.

An unsophisticated consumer needing credit has little bargaining power with the relatively small number of giant financial institutions (Citibank, Chase, Discover, HSBC) which dominate the credit card industry. Thus the contract is a "contract of adhesion" in which a gross inequity can be redressed by the court when that contract violates public policy or leads to an unconscionable result. *Santos v. Lumberman's Mutual Casualty* 408 Mass. 70.

Gross disparity in the values exchanged is an important fact to be considered in determining whether a contract in unconscionable . "Courts may avoid enforcement of a bargain that is shown to be unconscionable by reason of gross inadequacy of consideration accompanied by other relevant factors." Corbin Contracts §§ 128, at 551 [1963 and Supp. 1991] Moreover, an unconscionable contract is "such as no man in his sense and not under delusion would make on the one hand, and as no honest and fair man would accept on the other." *Hume v. United States* 132 U.S. 406, 411 (1889)

The charging of 30+% interest, though possibly legal, is so immoral that it contradicts the teachings of the three major religions. While scriptures hold no legal precedent, they can be morally instructive on the issue of conscionability.

In the Koran it is written that:

"O ye who believe! Fear Allah and give up what remains of your demand for usury if ye are indeed believers." 2:78

In the Old Testament it was written:

"If thou lend money to any of my people, even to the poor with thee, thou shalt not be to him as a creditor, neither shall ye lay upon him interest." Exodus 22:24

In the Sermon on the Mount, Jesus emphasizes lending without concern for a return:

"If ye lend to them of whom ye hope to receive, what thank have ye? For sinners also lend to sinners, to receive as much again. But love ye your enemies, and do good, and lend, hoping for nothing again..." Luke 6:35

The charging of 30.24% is unconscionable, offends public policy, and is so unfair as to shock the conscience.

Parties may disagree as to what is good public policy.

While some states such as Arkansas have placed caps on credit card interest, this state apparently has not. However, the "sub-prime" mortgage crisis is illustrative of the consequences of interest rate gouging. The Court in this case has the power to decide on the conscionability of this case, and to decide that public policy cannot tolerate the kind of overreaching that is represented by the conduct of the plaintiff. (See *Waters* above)

For all of these reasons, the Plaintiff's Motion for Summary Judgment should be denied.

Respectfully submitted,,

_____

Daniel and Diane Debtor

Dated: November 14, 2008

COMMONWEALTH OF MASSACHUSETTS

HAMPSHIRE, ss

DANA DISTRICT COURT
DOCKET NO.

FIRST PREDATOR BANK CARD OF)
SOUTH DAKOTA, N.A.)
      Plaintiff)
)
vs.)
)
DAN DEBTOR and DIANE DEBTOR,)
      Defendants)
)

AFFIDAVIT OF DANIEL DEBTOR

I, Daniel Debtor, being duly sworn and deposed, hereby do attest to the folowing:

1.   My name is Daniel Debtor. I, together with my wife Diane, am a defendant in this mater. I reside at 24 Elm Street, Daria, Massachusetts.

2.   On January 4, 2005, I entered into an agreement with the plaintiff to use its "Plastic Predator" card.

3.   On June 7, 2006 I sent in a check to the plaintiff which had the attached (Exhibit "A") endorsement to it.

4.   The plaintiff cashed the check and never notified me that they did not accept the new terms.

5.   Despite the conditions accepted, the plaintiff has continued colleciton action against me, causing me great inconvenience and pain of mind.

Signed under oath this _____ day of November, 2008.

_____
Daniel Debtor

RE: Addendum to Cardmember Agreement

ATTN: Revolving Account #

This is an addendum made to the terms of the cardmember agreement. The interest rate will be reduced to 0% per annum. The principal, if any, will be payable at a rate of $10 monthly. You agree not to sell or assign this account and rights for any claim to any third party. Any such action constitutes forfeiture of all rights and claims against me including litigation. No late charges or over limit charges will be billed to me. All previous late or over limit charges will be credited to this account. You understand that I may assign the benefits and rights of this agreement at any time to any third party. In regards to the arbitration provision, nothing in the cardmember agreement shall prevent me from seeking any and all remedies available to me in a court of law. Violation of these terms will constitute a material breach and a penalty of $10,000.00 shall be imposed for each and every material breach. Any future addendums or amendments shall also be made in writing and signed by both parties. For good consideration, a check/money order is enclosed. Cashing the enclosed check/money order constitutes acceptance and unequivocal assent to this adddendum/change/modification/ novation/counteroffer without recourse. If you do not agree wit these terms, you must notify me in writing 30 days from the date of this notice and return the attached check/money order for consideration uncashed.

MEMORANDUM OF DECISION AND ORDER ON PARTIES' CROSS-MOTIONS FOR SUMMARY JUDGMENT

COMMONWEALTH OF MASSACHUSETTS

ESSEX, ss.

**SUPERIOR COURT
CIVIL ACTION
NO. 09-02536-C**

CITIBANK (SOUTH DAKOTA), N.A.

<u>vs.</u>

ROSEMARY WALKER DECRISTOFORO

<u>MEMORANDUM OF DECISION AND ORDER ON PARTIES'
CROSS-MOTIONS FOR SUMMARY JUDGMENT</u>

INTRODUCTION

The plaintiff, Citibank (South Dakota), N.A. ("Citibank"), filed the current action for

account stated to recover a debt the defendant, Rosemary Walker DeCristoforo ("DeCristoforo"),

purportedly owes it with respect to two delinquent credit card accounts. In response,

DeCristoforo filed a counterclaim, alleging Citibank charged her interest in an amount greater

than allowed by federal law. The matter is currently before the court on the parties' cross-

motions for summary judgment. For the reasons explained below, DeCristoforo's Motion for

Partial Summary Judgment as to Liability on her Counterclaims will be **ALLOWED** in part and

Citibank's Cross-Motion for Summary Judgment will be **DENIED**.

BACKGROUND

A. Factual Background

The material facts do not appear to be in dispute. Citibank is a national banking association located in South Dakota. DeCristoforo is an individual residing in Beverly, Massachusetts.

On October 1, 1984, DeCristoforo opened a credit card line of credit with Citibank, which has a current account number ending in 8960 (the "1984 Account"). Almost ten years later, on March 14, 1994, DeCristoforo opened a second credit card line of credit with Citibank, which has a current account number ending in 6865 (the "1994 Account"). DeCristoforo used the 1984 and 1994 Accounts to obtain credit from Citibank to acquire goods, services, and/or cash advances.

Citibank mailed periodic billing statements for the 1984 and the 1994 Accounts to the address DeCristoforo provided. The last payment posted to the 1994 Account on August 14, 2008 in the amount of $316.15. The last payment posted to the 1984 Account on August 20, 2008 in the amount of $812.36. As of March 12, 2009, the outstanding balance on the 1994 Account, as reflected on its monthly statement, was $8,465.69. As of May 7, 2009, the outstanding balance on the 1984 Account, as reflected on its monthly statement, was $25,870.44.

With respect to all unpaid amounts owed under the 1984 Account, as asserted in monthly statements to DeCristoforo, dated January 8, 2001 thru May 7, 2009, Citibank charged interest at annual rates of no less than 14.4% and no greater than 32.24%, exclusive of late fees and other charges. With respect to all unpaid amounts owed under the 1994 Account, as asserted in monthly statements to DeCristoforo, dated July 13/August 13, 2001 thru February 12/March 12,

2009, Citibank charged interest at annual rates of no less than 10.65% and no greater than 54.7333%, exclusive of late fees and other charges.

B. The Consumer Credit Industry

Statistics show that DeCristoforo's circumstances are not unique. Twenty years ago, in 1990, there were approximately 82 million credit cardholders.[1] By 2003, that number had increased to 144 million.[2] In addition to an increase in the number of cardholders, there has been a 350% increase in the amount that these cardholders charge while, during the same period, income has only risen by 188%.[3] These statistics lead to the inescapable conclusion that the general public is drowning in credit card debt. In fact, almost 50% of American families owe some amount of credit card debt.[4] Importantly, these statistics are not just about "avid commercialism"—individuals are using credit cards for everyday necessities, such as food and utilities.[5] According to a report published in February 2008 by the Center for American Progress, in November 2007, total credit card debt in the United States had reached an all time high of $790.2 billion.[6] Sluggish economic recovery combined with the unregulated interest rates and hidden fees the credit card companies charge, however, make it impossible for

---

[1]   Susan Walker, *U.S. Consumer Credit Card Debt May Crash Economy*, FOX NEWS, Dec. 31, 2004, available at http://www.foxnews.com (last visited Dec. 17, 2010).

[2]   Id.

[3]   Id.

[4]   Brian K. Bucks, Arthur B. Kennickell, Trace L. Mach, & Kevin B. Moore, *Changes in U.S. Family Finances from 2004 to 2007: Evidence from the Survey of Consumer Finance*, FEDERAL RESERVE BULLETIN, vol. 95, Feb. 2009, available at http://www.federalreserve.gov (last visited Dec. 17, 2010).

[5]   See Christian E. Weller, *Warning: Credit Card Practices Can Be Detrimental to Your (and Their) Health*, CREDIT SLIPS: A DISCUSSION ON CREDIT, FINANCE, AND BANKRUPTCY, Mar. 19, 2009, available at http://www.creditslips.org (last visited Dec. 17, 2010) ("[People] would have to plaster walls with plasma [televisions], have [a] different ipod for every day, and rent storage for [their] new wardrobe[s] to explain [the] debt families have taken on in recent years.").

[6]   Tim Westrich & Christian E. Weller, *House of Cards: Consumers Turn to Credit Cards Amid the Mortgage Crisis, Delaying the Inevitable Defaults*, CENTER FOR AMERICAN PROGRESS, Feb. 2008, available at http://www.americanprogress.org (last visited Dec. 17, 2010).

consumers to get out from under these debts,[7] adversely impacting upon the ability of consumers to ever emerge from an endless interest and fees induced spiral.[8]

DISCUSSION

I.   Standard of Review

Summary judgment is appropriate where there are no genuine issues of material fact and the moving party is entitled to judgment as a matter of law. Mass. R. Civ. P. 56(c); Kourouvacilis v. General Motors Corp., 410 Mass. 706, 716 (1991). The moving party bears the burden of affirmatively showing that there is no triable issue of fact. Pederson v. Time, Inc., 404 Mass. 14, 16-17 (1989). The moving party may satisfy this burden either by submitting affirmative evidence that negates an essential element of the opposing party's case or by demonstrating that the opposing party has no reasonable expectation of proving an essential element of his case at trial. Flesner v. Technical Commc'ns Corp., 410 Mass. 805, 809 (1991). The nonmoving party cannot, however, defeat the well-pled motion for summary judgment by resting on its pleadings; rather, it must respond by alleging specific facts demonstrating the existence of a genuine fact. Correllas v. Viveiros, 410 Mass. 314, 317 (1991). The court views the evidence in the light most favorable to the nonmoving party, but does not weigh evidence, assess credibility, or find facts. Attorney Gen. v. Bailey, 386 Mass. 367, 370-371 (1982).

II.   DeCristoforo's Counterclaims

In support of summary judgment on her counterclaims, DeCristoforo argues 12 U.S.C. § 85 ("Section 85") caps interest at seven percent and that Citibank violated this provision by charging interest, on the 1984 Account, between 14.4% and 32.24%, and on the 1994 Account,

---

[7]   See Christian E. Weller, *Drowning in Debt: America's Middle Class Falls Deeper in Debt as Income Growth Slows and Costs Climb*, CENTER FOR AMERICAN PROGRESS, May 2006, available at http://www.americanprogress.org (last visited Dec. 17, 2010).

[8]   See Weller, CREDIT SLIPS, available at http://www.creditslips.org (last visited Dec. 17, 2010).

4

between 10.65% and 54.7333%. In response, Citibank contends Section 85 is not applicable in this case because, in accordance with the Supreme Court's holding in Daggs v. Pheonix Nat'l Bank, 177 U.S. 549 (1900), this provision only applies where the bank's home state does not allow for *any* interest. Since Citibank is headquarted in South Dakota and South Dakota allows interest at any rate agreed upon in writing, according to Citibank, it can charge interest at any rate agreed upon between it and its credit card customers. This dispute highlights an issue of national concern—mounting credit card debt and unregulated interest rates, which make paying that debt next to impossible.

A. Section 85

To help finance the Civil War, in 1861, then Treasury Secretary, Salmon P. Chase, recommended the federal government establish a national banking system whereby national banks could be chartered by the federal government and authorized to issue bank notes secured by government bonds.[9] This idea came to fruition a few years later, in 1864, when the National Banking Act was enacted.[10] Section 85 was included in the National Banking Act to protect against usurious interest rates.

Section 85 provides, in relevant part, that

> [a]ny association may . . . charge on any loan . . . or upon . . . other
> evidences of debt, interest at the rate allowed by the laws of the
> State . . . where the bank is located . . ., and no more, except that
> where by the laws of any State a different rate is limited for banks
> organized under State laws, the rate so limited shall be allowed for
> associations organized or existing in any such State under title 62
> of the Revised Statutes. When no rate is fixed by the laws of the
> State, . . . the bank may . . . charge a rate not exceeding 7 per
> centum . . . .

---

[9] Office of the Comptroller of the Currency, *History: The National Banking System*, UNITED STATES DEPARTMENT OF THE TREASURY, available at http://www.occ.treas.gov (last visited Dec. 17, 2010).

[10] Richard S. Grossman, *US Banking History: Civil War to World War II*, ECONOMIC HISTORY ASSOCIATION, Jan. 2, 2010, available at http://www.eh.net (last visited Dec. 17, 2010).

12 U.S.C. § 85. No decisions interpreting this provision, pertinent to the resolution of the current dispute, were decided until 1900 when the Supreme Court decided Daggs.

In Daggs, a national bank located in Arizona sought to enforce promissory notes bearing a ten percent interest rate. Id. at 549. In response, Daggs argued Section 85 limited the interest rate to seven percent, if no rate was "fixed" by the laws of the state or territory where the national bank was located. Id. at 554. Because, in Arizona, the interest rate was not "fixed" by the laws of the territory, but by the parties to the notes, Daggs contended the notes were usurious. Id. The Supreme Court disagreed. Id. at 555.

The Supreme Court concluded that the phrase "fixed by the laws," from the second sentence of Section 85, should be construed to mean "allowed by the laws." Id. It reasoned that the "national banks 'were established for the purpose, in part, of providing a currency for the whole country, and in part to create a market for the loans of the general government. It could not have been intended, therefore, to expose them to the hazard of unfriendly legislation by the states, or to ruinous competition with state banks.'" Id. at 555, quoting Tiffany v. National Bank, 85 U.S. 409, 413 (1873). Under this interpretation, Section 85's interest rate cap is only applicable when the laws of the bank's home state allow *no* interest rate. See Hawkins v. Citicorp Credit Servs., Inc., 665 F. Supp. 2d 518, 523 (2009) (emphasis added).

For all practical purposes, Daggs eliminated the protections afforded by Section 85. Following Daggs, the national banks were able to charge interest at whatever rate was allowed by the state in which they were located and there was very little uniformity from state to state. Interest rates were lower in states concerned with consumer protection, but much higher in states trying to lure large commercial banks into doing business within their borders. This went on

6

until 1978, when the Supreme Court decided <u>Marquette v. First Omaha Serv. Corp.</u>, 439 U.S. 299 (1978).

<u>Marquette</u> involved two banks: Marquette National Bank of Minneapolis ("Marquette"), where the state's usury law capped interest rates for loans at twelve percent; and the First National Bank of Omaha ("First National") in Nebraska, where state laws allowed an interest rate of up to eighteen percent. <u>Id</u>. at 301-303. To make up for the low cap in Minnesota, banks in Minnesota could charge an annual fee, which Marquette did. <u>Id</u>. at 304-305. First National then started marketing its credit cards to Minnesota residents as "no-fee" cards. <u>Id</u>.

Perceiving itself to be at a disadvantage, Marquette sued First National, arguing it was violating Minnesota's usury law. <u>Id</u>. The Supreme Court made two important rulings. First, it concluded that state usury laws do not apply to nationally chartered banks based in other states. See <u>id</u> at 308. Second, it decided that nationally chartered banks can "export" the interest rates allowed in their home states to customers throughout the country. <u>Id</u>. at 313-314. Under this holding, when a bank from a state without limits on interest issues credit cards to people living in states, which cap credit card interest, the costumer can be charged any rate of interest. See <u>id</u>.

The <u>Marquette</u> decision caused unprecedented expansion in the consumer credit industry as large national banks relocated to states with lender-friendly interest rate provisions.[11] Today, all of the major credit card companies are located in a handful of states such as South Dakota, Utah, Arizona, and Delaware where the interest rate caps are either extremely high or nonexistent.[12] Citibank is no exception.

---

[11] Pat Curry, *How a Supreme Court Ruling Killed Off Usury Laws for Credit Card Rates: A 1978 Court Case Changed the Industry—and Put Cards in Everyone's Pocket*, FOX NEWS, Nov. 12, 2010, available at http://www.foxbusiness.com (last visited Dec. 17, 2010).

[12] Frontline, *Secret History of the Credit Card: Map: Snapshot of the Industry*, FRONTLINE, Nov. 23, 2004, available at http://www.pbs.org/wgbh/pages/frontline/shows/credit/more/map.html (last visited Dec. 17, 2010).

In 1980, during a time of great economic strife in South Dakota, Citibank executives approached the then governor, William Janklow, with a plan.[13] Citibank would move its headquarters to South Dakota, providing hundreds of high-paying white-collar jobs, if South Dakota quickly passed legislation eliminating its interest rate cap.[14] South Dakota responded by passing a new interest rate provision, which provides, in pertinent part, that

> [u]nless a maximum interest rate or charge is specifically
> established elsewhere in the code, there is no maximum interest
> rate or charge, or usury rate restriction, between or among persons,
> corporations, . . . associations, or any other entities if they establish
> the interest rate or charge by written agreement. A written
> agreement includes the contract created by § 54-11-9.[15]

South Dakota Condified Laws § 54-3-1. Thereafter, Citibank relocated from New York to South Dakota.[16] Ultimately, this arrangement succeeded beyond the parties' expectations. Citibank's agreement with South Dakota brought 3,000 high-paying jobs to the state and enabled Citibank to become a credit card giant, exporting South Dakota's unregulated interest rate provision to customers around the country, including DeCristoroforo.[17] Merely because Citibank is able to charge interest premised on South Dakota law, which does not cap interest, does not, however, mean Citibank can charge *any* interest rate. Citibank's interest rate must still comport with common law concepts of fairness such as unconscionability.[18]

---

[13] Robin Stein, *Secret History of the Credit Card: The Assendancy of the Credit Card Industry*, FRONTLINE, Nov. 23, 2004, available at http://www.pbs.org/wgbh/pages/frontline/shows/credit/more/rise.html (last visited Dec. 17, 2010).

[14] Id.

[15] South Dakota Codified Laws § 54-11-9 provides that "[t]he use of an accepted credit card or the issuance of a credit card agreement . . . creates a binding contract between the card holder and the card issuer with reference to any accepted card, and any charges made with the authorization of the primary card holder."

[16] Stein, available at http://www.pbs.org/wgbh/pages/frontline/shows/credit/more/rise.html (last visited Dec. 17, 2010).

[17] Id.

[18] Below, the court addresses unconscionability. As an initial matter, however, the court notes that Massachusetts law applies to its unconscionability analysis. In determining what law applies, the court must use the

B. Unconscionability

"The doctrine of unconscionability has long been recognized by common law courts in this country and in England." Waters v. Min Ltd., 412 Mass. 64, 66 (1992), and cases cited. As the Appeals Court aptly explained more than three decades ago:

> Historically, a bargain was considered unconscionable if it was
> 'such as no man in his senses and not under delusion would make
> on the one hand, and as no honest and fair man would accept on
> the other.' Hume v. United States, 132 U.S. 406[, 411] (1889),
> quoting 38 Eng. Rep. 82, 100 (Ch. 1750). Later, a contract was
> determined unenforceable because unconscionable when 'the sum
> total of its provisions drives too hard a bargain for a court of
> conscience to assist.' Campbell Soup Co. v. Wentz, 172 F.2d 80,
> 84 (3rd Cir. 1948).

Covich v. Chambers, 8 Mass. App. Ct. 740, 750 n.13 (1979).

Unconscionability is a matter of law decided by the court and must be determined on a case-by-case basis. Zapatha v. Dairy Mart, Inc., 381 Mass. 284, 291 (1980). Particular attention is addressed to "whether the challenged provision could result in oppression and unfair surprise to the disadvantaged party." Waters, 412 Mass. at 68, quoting Zapatha, 381 Mass. at 292-293.

---

conflict-of-law rules of the forum state, i.e., Massachusetts. See Clarendon Nat'l Ins. Co. v. Arbella Mut. Ins. Co., 60 Mass. App. Ct. 492, 495 (2004). Massachusetts has adopted a functional choice-of-law approach to contract cases that "responds to the interests of the parties, the [s]tates involved, and the interstate system as a whole." Bushkin Assoc., Inc. v. Raytheon Co., 393 Mass. 622, 631 (1985). "Under this approach, in the absence of a contractually binding choice of law clause or agreement, [the] court looks to the law of the state with the most significant relationship to the transaction and the parties." Spence v. Kantrovitz, 392 F. Supp. 2d 29, 35 (D. Mass. 2005) (footnote omitted); see also Restatement (Second) of Conflict of Laws, § 6 (1971). In determining which state has the most significant relationship, the court examines "(a) the needs of the interstate and international systems, (b) the relevant policies of the forum, (c) the relevant policies of other interested states and the relative interests of those states in the determination of the particular issue, (d) the protection of justified expectations, (e) the basic policies underlying the particular field of law, (f) certainty, predictability and uniformity of result, and (g) ease in the determination and application of the law to be applied." Bushkin, Assocs., Inc., 393 Mass. at 632, citing Restatement (Second) of Conflict of Laws, § 6(2) (1971).

In this case, the parties have not provided the court with a contract identifying a choice of law provision. Thus, the court must use the factors set forth in the Restatement to determine whether South Dakota or Massachusetts has the most significant relationship to the transactions at issue. None of the above factors weigh in favor of applying South Dakota law. Citbank purposely chooses to market its credit card products to Massachusetts residents. DeCristoforo is a resident of Massachusetts. Any contract or agreement between Citibank and DeCristoforo would have been executed in Massachusetts. Most importantly, Massachusetts has a strong public policy interest in ensuring its residents are protected against predatory lending practices, which is more significant than any countervailing interest South Dakota may have in the current dispute.

"'The principle is one of prevention of oppression . . . and not of disturbance of [the] allocation of risks because of superior bargaining power.'" Zapatha, 381 Mass. at 292, quoting U.C.C. § 2-302, cmt. 1. "Oppression" is a matter of the substantive unfairness of the contract; "unfair surprise" means procedural unfairness in the manner in which the contract was concluded." See id. at 293-295.

Substantive unconscionability occurs when contract terms are unreasonably favorable to one party. See Gilman v. Chase-Manhattan Bank, N.A., 534 N.E.2d 824, 829 (N.Y. 1988) (stating the question of substantive unconscionability "entails an analysis of the substance of the bargain to determine whether the terms were unreasonably favorable to the party against whom the unconscionability is urged . . . ."). When "a provision of the contract is so outrageous as to warrant holding it unenforceable," unconscionability can be based on the substantive component alone. Id. Meanwhile, procedural unconscionability "requires an examination of the contract formation process and the alleged lack of meaningful choice." Id. at 828.

Although the facts pertaining to the formation of DeCristorforo's credit card agreements are not set forth in the record, the court can fully grasp the one-sided nature of those proceedings. Nevertheless, even putting procedural unconscionability aside, the court concludes this is an instance where unconscionability can be based on the substantive component alone. Id. at 829. The court acknowledges that Citibank's interest rate charges are not always unreasonable. For example, at times, Citibank charged DeCristoforo as little at 10.65%. As time went by, however, Citibank continually increased its rate, especially as DeCristoforo began to fall behind with her payments, until it reached rates as high as 54.7333%. Substantial interest rate hikes such as this have greatly contributed the consumer credit crisis in America.

With interest rates as high as forty and fifty percent, a significant portion of the debtor's monthly payment goes toward paying interest without touching the underlying debt. At these rates, individuals must make monthly payments for years before putting a dent in their debt, especially when one owes credit balances in excess of $25,000, as is the case with DeCristoforo. Interest charges at these rates drain needed resources and slow economic growth. Citibank's charges, in excess of eighteen percent, "drives too hard a bargain for a court of conscience to assist." Campbell Soup Co., 172 F.2d at 84. The court concludes interest rate charges above eighteen percent are unconscionable and "so outrageous as to warrant holding [them] . . . unenforceable." Gilman, 534 N.E.2d at 829.

III.   Citibank's Claims

Citibank contends it is entitled to summary judgment on its account stated claims because it mailed monthly statements for both the 1984 and the 1994 Accounts to DeCristoforo, showing the transactions on those accounts, and she retained these statements without objecting to the charges. In response, DeCristoforo argues there is an issue of fact as to whether her failure to object to the accuracy of the statements constitutes an acknowledgment of their correctness. The court concludes summary judgment is inappropriate because there is no agreement between the parties as to what DeCristoforo owes Citibank.

"'A stated account is an agreement between the parties entered into after an examination of the items by which a balance is struck in favor of one of them . . . .'" Davis v. Arnold, 267 Mass. 103, 110 (1929), quoting McMahon v. Brown, 219 Mass. 23, 27 (1914). A claim for account stated does not create liability where non existed previously; rather, it determines the amount of a debt where liability already exists. Id., citing Chase v. Chase, 119 Mass. 556 (1876). Under an account stated theory, a party's receipt of account statements and the failure to

11

timely object to the amounts reflected establishes the party's liability for the account balance. See Milliken v. Warwick, 306 Mass. 192, 196-197 (1940) (stating assent "'may be inferred from the reception and retaining of the account without objection'"), quoting Union Bank v. Knapp, 3 Pick 96, 113 (1825); see also McMahon, 219 Mass. at 27.

Here, it is undisputed that Citibank mailed, to DeCristoforo, monthly statements for the 1984 and the 1994 Accounts. Further, DeCristoforo does not appear to dispute that she made the purchases or accepted the cash advances listed on the account statements. At an initial glance this would seem to support summary judgment in Citibank's favor. However, in her counterclaim, which is discussed above, DeCristoforo objects to the interest rate Citibank charged. Although DeCristoforo is clearly liable for the goods, services, and/or cash advances she incurred under each account, there is no agreement between the parties as to what DeCristoforo actually owes Citibank. Therefore, Citibank's Cross-Motion for Summary Judgment will be **DENIED**.

ORDER

For the reasons set forth above, it is hereby **ORDERED** that: (1) DeCristoforo's Motion for Partial Summary Judgment is **ALLOWED** in relation to interest charged by Citibank; and (2) Citibank's Cross-Motion for Summary Judgment is **DENIED**. The parties are further **ORDERED** to appear before this court on February 10, 2011 at 2:00 p.m. for a status conference and an assessment of damages hearing.

SO ORDERED.

Date: January 4, 2011

Robert A. Cornetta
Justice

APPENDIX "I"

REQUESTS FOR ADMISSION PROPOUNDED BY THE DEFENDANT TO THE PLAINTIFF

COMMONWEALTH OF MASSACHUSETTS

Norfolk, ss

Quincy District Court
Civil Docket No.
(Transfer from Small Claim Docket No.)

▓▓▓▓▓▓▓▓▓▓▓▓▓▓▓▓	)
Plaintiff	)
	)
v.	)
	)
▓▓▓▓▓▓▓▓▓▓▓▓	)
Defendant	)
	)

REQUESTS FOR ADMISSION PROPOUNDED BY THE DEFENDANT TO THE PLAINTIFF (FIRST SET)

Pursuant to the Massachusetts Rules of Civil Procedure, the following matters of which admissions are requested are deemed admitted unless you reply in writing when 30 days with a proper denial or objection.

1.   Admit that the date on which the defendant's account allegedly went into default was more than six years prior to the date you serviced Defendant with the Summons and Complaint.

2.   Admit that there was no written agreement signed by the defendant, incorporating the terms and conditions of any agreement you allege exists in the case.

3.   Admit that there is no agreement between you and the defendant.

4.   Admit that the defendant has not received noticed of any assignment of the account.

5.   Admit that the Defendant has not consented to any assignment of the account.

6.   Admit that the Defendant has not waived notice of assignment of the account.

7.   Admit that Defendant has not ratified any assignment of the account.

8.   Admit that as of the date you drafted your complaint you had no evidence admissible at trial that proves Defendant owes the debt.

9.   Admit that you are not the real party in interest.

10.   Admit that your predecessor entered into an accord and satisfaction, or novation, by means of cashing a check with a restrictive endorsement.

By his attorney,

_____
David C. Grossack, Esquire
Suite 103
1320 Centre St.
Newton, MA 02459
(617) 965-9300

Dated: July 26, 2011

**FIRST SET OF INTERROGATORIES PROPOUNDED BY THE DEFENDANT
TO THE PLAINTIFF**

COMMONWEALTH OF MASSACHUSETTS

Norfolk, ss

Quincy District Court
Civil Docket No.
(Transfer from Small Claim Docket No.)

```
                                    )
 ▓▓▓▓▓▓▓▓▓▓▓▓▓▓▓▓▓▓▓▓▓▓▓▓▓▓▓▓        )
        Plaintiff                   )
                                    )
            v.                      )
                                    )
 ▓▓▓▓▓▓▓▓▓▓▓▓▓▓▓▓▓▓                  )
        Defendant                   )
                                    )
```

FIRST SET OF INTERROGATORIES PROPOUNDED BY THE DEFENDANT TO THE PLAINTIFF

1.   Kindly identify each and every person participating in the response to the interrogatories by name, address and employment title.

2.   Please identify the date the plaintiff purportedly acquired title to defendant's account and the consideration paid for the account.

3.   What interest rate is the plaintiff charging the defendant?

4.   Please identify each and every collection agency which handled defendant's account prior to this action being commenced.

5.   Do any sound recordings exist of conversations with the defendant by any collectors who worked on his account?

6.   If the answer to the previous interrogatory is in the affirmative, please fully identify each recording and its custodian.

7.   Identify and describe each and every step taken by all persons who worked on the defendant's account on behalf of the plaintiff. Please explain all of the activities they engaged in, who witnessed said activities, and state whether or not phone calls with the defendant were recorded.

8.   Please identify the individuals by name and residential address who had supervisory authority over the defendant's account.

9.   Identify every person who has or may have personal knowledge of the claims, defenses or allegations in this lawsuit, including all persons you may call as a witness at trial.

10.   Identify all documents you claim demonstrate Defendant's consent to be obligated on the account.

11.   Identify all prior owners or assignees of the account, including all previous or alternate names of each owner or assignee, and state the date of each assignment.

12.   State the date or dates on which Defendant was notified of each sale or assignment of the account.

13.   Identify every person with a legal, equitable or beneficial interest in the account.

14.   If you contend that any relevant documents have been lost or destroyed, state for each document:

> (a)   Whether the document was lost or destroyed.
>
> (b)   The date the document was lost or destroyed.
>
> (c)   If destroyed, the method of destruction, and
> (d)   If destroyed, identify the person who ordered the destruction.

15.   Describe all methods, practices, procedures or systems used to track the account since it was opened.

16.   Describe all practices, processes and systems in place to protect against clerical error and ensure the accuracy of the account since it was opened.

17.   Identify all documents in your possession or control related to this account which contain Defendant's signature, and/or the signature of ███████████████
███████████████

By his attorney,

_____

David C. Grossack, Esquire
Suite 103
1320 Centre St.
Newton, MA 02459
(617) 965-9300

Dated: July 26, 2011

APPENDIX "K"

DEFENDANT'S MOTION TO COMPEL RESPONSE TO REQUEST FOR PRODUCTION OF DOCUMENTS

COMMONWEALTH OF MASSACHUSETTS

Norfolk, ss

Quincy District Court
Civil Docket No. ▓▓▓▓▓▓▓▓▓

```
                                )
▓▓▓▓▓▓▓▓▓▓▓▓▓▓▓▓▓▓▓              )
        Plaintiff               )
                                )
        v.                      )
                                )
▓▓▓▓▓▓▓▓▓▓▓▓                    )
        Defendant               )
                                )
                                )
```

DEFENDANT'S MOTION TO COMPEL RESPONSE TO REQUEST FOR PRODUCTION OF DOCUMENTS

Now comes the defendant by counsel and moves that this court compel the defendant to respond to the document request serviced upon it on July 26, 2011. (Ex "A)

Defendant states that each and every item sought is relevant to issues which will be raised at trial and is calculated to lead to admissible evidence.

Defendant states that 30 days have passed, and the plaintiff has not produced any documents.

Wherefore defendant prays this court (a) order the plaintiff to produce the documents within 5 business days and (b) order the plaintiff to pay the reasonable attorney's fees associated with this motion.

by his attorney,

David C. Grossack, Esquire
Suite 103
1320 Centre St.
Newton, MA 02459
(617) 965-9300

APPENDIX "L"

DEFENDANT'S REQUEST FOR PRODUCTION OF DOCUMENTS

COMMONWEALTH OF MASSACHUSETTS

Norfolk, ss

Quincy District Court
Civil Docket No.
(Transfer from Small Claim Docket No.)

▆▆▆▆▆▆▆▆▆▆	)
Plaintiff	)
	)
	)
v.	)
	)
▆▆▆▆▆▆▆▆	)
Defendant	)
	)

DEFENDANT'S REQUEST FOR PRODUCTION OF DOCUMENTS

Now comes the defendant by counsel pursuant to Rule 34 MRCP, and requests that the plaintiff produce each and every document listed in the accompanying Schedule "A".

▆▆▆▆▆▆▆▆▆▆
By his attorney,

David C. Grossack, Esquire
Suite 103
1320 Centre St.
Newton, MA 02459
(617) 965-9300
▆▆▆▆▆▆

Dated: July 26, 2011

COMMONWEALTH OF MASSACHUSETTS

Norfolk, ss

Quincy District Court
Civil Docket No.
(Transfer from Small Claim Docket No.)

)
)
Plaintiff)
)
)
v.)
)
)
)
Defendant)
)

SCHEDULE "A"

1. Each and every written agreement between the parties, or your alleged predecessor in interest.

2. Any and all credit card charge slips, statements of account and invoices relating to the defendant, in your possession or scope of control.

3. Any and all training manuals, memos, directives or other graphically recorded communications concerning the processing of checks with restrictive endorsements by mail handlers at plaintiff corporation's predecessor in interest.

4. Any and all documents reflecting any assignment of defendant's alleged debt to the plaintiff.

5. Any and all certificates of corporate vote authorizing this action.

6. Any and all records of payments made by the defendant to plaintiff and/or its predecessor in interest.

7. Any internal policy or procedure manuals, memos or directive concerning checks with restrictive language.

8. Any and all documents listing the names and addresses of each and every person employed by the plaintiff who handles checks mailed to the plaintiff.

9. Any and all written communications between the parties.

10. Any and all agreements and correspondence exchanged between plaintiff and its predecessor in interest concerning the acquisition of the account in question.

11. Any and all copies of checks and/or correspondence from Court Mediation Services.

By his attorney,

David C. Grossack, Esquire
Suite 103
1320 Centre St.
Newton, MA 02459
(617) 965-9300

Dated: July 26, 2011

www.ingramcontent.com/pod-product-compliance
Lightning Source LLC
Chambersburg PA
CBHW082110210326

41599CB00033B/6660